THE A
FROM HUMAN
BEHAVIOR

The New Strongest Argument

Eric Demaree

All Biblical references are from the King James Version of the Bible (KJV). Some words and phrases have been modernized.

Published by

Fellowship Books
POB 252
Kingman AZ 86402
USA

CONTENTS

FOREWORD

Although I have known Eric Demaree for more than ten years, I was still surprised to find that he seems to have discovered one of the most persuasive street-wise arguments for God that I have seen. In this thought-provoking book, Eric reveals his masterful ability to discover heretofore unknown truths and articulate the difficult study of God's existence.

As a philosopher, I was awed by his Argument from Human Behavior. It is strong enough that Eric makes the case for God's existence to be declared scientifically probable because, he argues, we all have indirect perceptions of God when we take our sense of "wrong" seriously.

His religious narrative, Christian Objectivism, is both simple and comprehensive. Its entire theology is derived from only one directive—Be reasonable. Someday it could possibly be called "The Theology of Everything" because, drawing from Einstein's ideas, it attempts to unify God and faith and science and reason.

This book is a must read for everyone who wants a solid understanding of the "God who is," which begins with what He has written into our conscience. I believe "The Argument from Human Behavior" and Christian Objectivism will clear the air about religions because they are reason's most perceptive assault on, not only atheism, but also on religious absurdities.

Tom K. Lee
Adjunct Professor of Philosophy, Retired

INTRODUCTION

The Argument from Human Behavior has exceptional force because if our hard-to live-by sense of "wrong" (our sense of everyone's moral obligations) came from evolution, then why do we ALL take at least part of that sense of "wrong" seriously, as if it were authored by God, and enforced by God?

This Argument is the strongest argument for God yet because it enables any thinking person to achieve the "certainty unto death" that God exists. More than a few martyrs have followed, sometimes subconsciously, a definite rational certainty into martyrdom for God. This argument, *for the first time,* verbalizes that rationale.

Nobody, ABSOLUTELY NO ONE, would say to God on His Judgment Day: You should not punish me because it was impossible for me to achieve the certainty You existed. No one would be able to out-argue God about not being able to know of His existence. Consequently, if the Biblical God exists, then a slam-dunk argument for Him must exist also!

Furthermore, the Bible prophesies in Hebrews 8:11 that a slam-dunk argument for God assuredly will be discovered! This verse says: And they shall not teach every man his neighbor and every man his brother, saying: Know the Lord. For ALL shall know me from the least to the greatest.

Three qualities of "The Argument from Human Behavior" make it superior to other arguments for God. First, this argument discovers a universal indirect perception of God that everyone has many times every day: the fact that we all take seriously our sense of "wrong." Second, this argument reveals that the Biblical God claims He is the legislator of the moral laws in our mind. Third, it understands that discovering God will always demand a step of faith; thus making an objective proof of God unattainable. However, the fact that we all have perceptions of God produces the extreme probability, and the inductive certainty, that God exists.

This book is philosophically precise, however, it is still accessible to non-philosophers. Everyone who is willing to stop and think should readily understand the Simplified Argument. The Superior Argument may be difficult reading for some, however, only thinking things over is needed to grasp it.

This book will also give you a basic understanding of the theory of knowledge, the philosophy of science and, perhaps, even your own personality. It will be a great blessing to you if are a seeker who is willing to do just a little thinking because this book contains the ultimate religious argument as well as the ultimate religious narrative—Christian Objectivism.

While writing this book many at the God-in-me Ministries of Las Vegas were supportive and helpful in giving me feedback on my work, especially Tom K. Lee. I would like to thank them for helping me prepare this book for publication. Most of all, I thank God for giving me tremendous joy while writing this book, which is the greatest reward. Thanks to Him for that!

SECTION I -
THE ARGUMENT FROM HUMAN BEHAVIOR

We will not find God with a telescope, but when we look within ourselves—there He is!

This section introduces an extremely persuasive argument for God: The Argument from Human Behavior. This radically fresh argument asks the question: Why do we all take our hard-to-live-by sense of "wrong," no matter how eroded, seriously? It answers that we can only take our sense of "wrong" seriously if we presuppose God's existence.

The essays in this section attempt to discover scientific certainties about God's existence. They are built on C. S. Lewis's ideas, especially the ideas in his book, *Mere Christianity*. I believe that the essays here are similar to what C. S. Lewis would have written if he had taken his studies a step further. These essays also stand on Alvin Plantinga's ideas, which reveal that because of our experiences we do not need an argument to have a reasonable belief in God.[1]

Although the philosophy journal editors who have seen parts of this argument endorse them as impressive, thought-provoking and a quality work, many non-philosophers fail to do enough thinking. Their environment has programmed their minds with the idea that it is impossible to achieve scientific certainties about God. However, the Biblical God *demands* that everyone achieve the "scientific certainty" He exists. No one will protest God's judgment by saying that it was impossible for him or her to achieve the certainty He existed. If the Biblical God does exist, then the certainty He exists must follow! God would not be justified in a Judgment Day if achieving the certainty of His existence was not accessible to everyone.

---

[1]Plantinga, A., 2000, *Warranted Christian Belief*, New York: Oxford University Press.

1

It is highly improbable that every one of the billions, who believe in God, is an irrational, wishful thinker. So where could rational belief in God originate? When most people think of rational belief in God, they think of evidence from physics or astronomy. They think that if God cannot be discovered through physical or astronomical means, He cannot be discovered. However, other evidence exists. This evidence is our sense of "wrong" and is the *only* evidence that could possibly validate our belief in a "God who demands morality." If we did discover God through astronomy, we still would not know whether or not He demanded morality.

The essence of my argument is—we *must* presuppose God's existence in order to take any part of our sense of "wrong" seriously. Everyone takes some "wrongs" seriously, even if he or she has almost completely fabricated his or her idea of "wrong." I conclude that because of the fact everyone takes "wrong" seriously, God's existence is written into everyone's mind, just as the Biblical God promises to do.

The template for the Argument from Human Behavior:

Premise 1: We all take seriously at least part of our sense of "wrong" (our sense of everyone's moral obligations).

Premise 2: If we take seriously even part of our sense of "wrong," then we have, in our mind, perceptions of God's existence.

Conclusion: Therefore, we all have, in our mind, perceptions of God's existence.

(Premise 1 is substantiated through observing **human behavior**.)

It is highly unlikely that an outlandish quirk of evolution put perceptions of God's existence into everyone's mind. On the other hand, it is *extremely probable* that the Biblical God put perceptions of His existence into everyone's mind, just as He promised to do in Hebrews 10:16: This is the covenant I will make with them after those days, saith the Lord, I will put my laws into their hearts and in their minds will I write them.

However, there could be any number of reasons, besides God, why we take "wrong" seriously. Thus, this argument now turns into a "checkmate" type of argument. This argument, in order to be sound, must eliminate every possibility of how we could take "wrong" seriously without needing God to exist. It must cut off every escape route. The following essays examine every escape from this checkmate.

These essays do NOT argue that morality comes from God. They do NOT even argue God exists! They DO argue, however, that God exists in everyone's mind. That is, they argue that we cannot take "wrong" seriously unless we have presupposed God's existence. These essays also DO argue that the fact everyone presupposes God's existence, is enough evidence to declare God's existence scientifically probable.

The foundation for the inquiry into God's existence begins with these two questions: (1) Do we have perceptions of God? And (2) do our perceptions produce scientific certainties? If the answer to both these questions is "yes," then God's existence would be scientifically probable. Just a "yes" answer to these two simple questions verifies God's existence.

If our sense of "wrong" gives us all indirect perceptions of God, then God's existence would be scientifically probable because all scientific facts arise from our perceptions. God's existence would never be an objective fact, but nonetheless, a scientific probability and possibly a scientific certainty.

I am now asking you, dear reader, to do a substantial amount of thinking! Think things over until you are certain that an escape exists or that no escape exists from this argument. Search your heart until you find that you need, or do not need, to presuppose God's existence in order to take your sense of "wrong" seriously. That is, I am asking you to think through, to its conclusion, this all-important question— Why is it that we all take our hard-to-live-by sense of "wrong," no matter how eroded, so seriously?

3

God made it easy for doubters to deny Him because it is easy *not* to do the thinking and the heart-searching needed to discover His existence.

SOME SIMPLE ARGUMENTS AND QUESTIONS

The ideas in the following paragraphs are practical and effective in helping people realize that they have perceptions of God. They provoke most people to think over their reasons for rejecting God's existence and convince some to take the step of faith to acknowledge His existence. That needed step of faith is the step of trusting that our seriously taken sense of "wrong" accurately reveals what exists. Since acknowledging God's existence will always require that step of faith, the questions here are often more effective than arguments in helping doubters to think things over.

Suppose a sales clerk lied to you without breaking the law. How do you know this act is seriously "wrong?" How do you know "survival of the fittest" does not apply here? Likewise, how do you know, without so much as a second thought, that the sales clerk is not just more evolved than you are? You can only *know* this act is seriously "wrong" if you assume God wrote, "lying is wrong." into your mind. If you assumed a human source wrote it into your mind, you would understand it to be just someone's opinion and not truth. If you assumed evolution wrote it into your mind, you would understand it to be nonsense and not truth. You would understand that constantly evolving evolution would just be playing a short-term trick on you. However, the idea "lying is wrong" is so deep-seated that even professing atheists behave as if it is God's truth. Thus, everyone's behavior is based on the presumption that God exists.

Here is a sample dialogue:

Doubter: "That salesman lied to me and cheated me!"

4

Believer: "Why is that "wrong?" Who made lying "wrong?" Evolution? According to evolution, lying makes that salesman better adapted to survive and more advanced than you are. You could only feel "wronged" if you subconsciously assumed God wrote "lying is wrong" into your mind. Otherwise, you would understand that you were simply defeated by "survival of the fittest". You say you do not believe in God, however, *only* if God is alive in your mind is lying seriously "wrong."

Only God has the authority to decree an action to be "wrong." Further, only He is able to enforce "wrong" and thereby keep it from evolving into an unenforced absurdity. Everyone who takes any part of their sense of "wrong" seriously, *behaves as if God exists*. Take a step of faith and trust that your sense of "wrong" accurately reveals what actually exists—God."

The ensuing statements are more evidence of universal belief in God. As Dostoevsky suggested, if God were dead everything would be permitted. If no God exists and this world is all there is, then why would dictators not be permitted to kill others in order to obtain luxuries and power? If no God exists they would essentially be following the evolutionary directive, "survival of the fittest," and furthering an always evolving human moral code.

Just as sure as "wrong" is absolutely wrong, God exists. Is it absolutely wrong for dictators to kill people in order to obtain luxuries and power? Or, does the slightest possibility exist that our sense of "wrong" is an illusion created by evolution? If it is absolutely wrong for dictators to murder, then God exists.

Why does everyone know that belief in God demands morality? Atheists will criticize someone who claims to believe in God but is immoral. Even atheists have indirect perceptions of God through their sense of "wrong."

Is our conscience an absurdity because it gives us directives with no enforcer of those directives? Unenforced directives are absurdities, as in: if you break this law, there is no penalty. If our conscience is worthy of being followed, then God must exist to enforce its directives. If God does not exist and our conscience evolved, then its directives are always changing and unenforceable. Our conscience would then be an absurdity and not ever be worthy to be followed!

Everyone who *attaches importance* to morality by saying, "I can be moral without God," is behaving as if God exists. Only God's existence is authoritative enough to stop morality's importance from being devalued to nonsense. Furthermore, people can indeed be moral without God but they have no reason, without God's existence, to be moral. If God did not exist, being moral would not matter at all. If God did not exist, why would I keep any promises? As John Locke argued, breaking promises would give me more of everything. If God did not exist, why would I care about others? They're not me! In addition, if God did not exist, whatever happens—so what? We would all soon die and disappear forever anyway. As a result, if God did not exist *nothing* else would matter!

Furthermore, almost all of us have "justice is necessary" written into our minds. Whether our ideas of justice are reasonable or unreasonable, most of us demand justice when we think we have been wronged. Why do we demand justice? Complete, true justice, as it is written into our minds, cannot possibly exist unless God exists and has a Judgment Day planned. Throughout history, for example, thousands of murderers have never been brought to justice. Has a sadistic twist of evolution made us crave something that could never possibly exist? Or, did God Himself write His justice into our minds just as the Biblical God promises to do?

When I tell doubters about God, I do not answer their diversionary questions. Instead, I ask them questions in order to help them think things over. Here are some questions I have used to convince my atheist companions that God exists.

When one of them complains someone has lied to him, I ask: "Who made lying wrong?" or, "Why are you taking the directive, 'Do not lie,' so seriously if it came from evolution and could be invalidated at any time by evolving again?" or, "How do you know with such certainty the person who lied to you is not actually more resourceful in surviving than you are?" When my companions are confronted by questions like these, some make frivolous rebuttals, some stop and say nothing, however, a few take a step of faith and acknowledge God's existence. If I meet a hateful person, I often reply, "Why are you hateful? You know hate is wrong because God wrote that into your mind. Do you think God would go to the trouble of writing "hate is wrong" into your mind and then not enforce it?"

THE PRELIMINARY ARGUMENT

The following is an introductory argument. It is an accurate and detailed description of the phenomenon: belief in God. It attempts to establish that God's existence could be a scientific fact,[2] although *never* an objective fact. It does not conclude: God is alive; instead, it concludes that God is alive in

---

[2] Ayn Rand, *Introduction to Objectivist Epistemology*, 40-54. Derived from Rand's definitions, I define "fact" as a true certainty achieved through previous experiences in conjunction with faith—faith in inductive reasoning, faith in naïve realism (faith that our senses accurately reveal what actually exists) or faith in the uniformity of nature (faith that the laws of Physics will continue to be valid). Experiences also determine whether a certainty is a fact and a true certainty or a "hasty generalization" and a false certainty. Additionally, those who have achieved true certainties through reason are able to achieve the true certainty that those who have achieved certainties through rationalizations have achieved false certainties.

7

everyone's mind. Acknowledging God's existence will *always* demand a step of faith. In order to make this argument easier to understand, I needed to omit some supporting statements. If you have any questions or doubts about this argument, before concluding anything, go on to the complete Superior Argument. Here is the simpler argument:

Premise 1: Everyone considers, at least, one action to be "wrong."

Premise 2: We cannot consider any action to be "wrong" unless God is alive in our minds.

Conclusion: Therefore, God is alive in everyone's mind.

Corollary: Either evolution wrote God's existence into everyone's mind or God Himself did it.

Explanations—Premise 1: Everyone considers, at least, one action to be "wrong." Everyone, whether using crooked thinking or not, behaves as if at least one action is "wrong" and behaves as if this wrong should be taken seriously. Everyone, for example, behaves as if some type of lying or some type of murder is seriously wrong.

Premise 2: We cannot consider any action to be "wrong" unless God is alive in our minds. The rightness or wrongness everyone attaches to human actions would be nonsense if God did not author *and* enforce these normative valuations. No one else has the authority to decree right and wrong. In like manner, no one else has the power to enforce right and wrong. Every seriously taken valuation of "wrong" presupposes God. If God were not alive in our minds, for example, we would consider lying the smartest thing to do because of the advantages we would have in getting things from others. We would also consider the directive "do not lie" nonsense because we would understand it to be either from evolution or from a human source and, thus, unenforceable.

If we assumed the idea "wrong" came through evolution, we would attach no importance to it because we would understand that our ideas of "wrong" could evolve into different ideas at any time. If we assumed the idea "wrong"

8

came from a human source we would understand it to be just someone's opinion and we would not take it seriously.

If we assumed the idea "wrong" came from a person, we would take that person seriously but we would not take the idea "wrong" seriously. A few people, for example, believe some ideas of "wrong" come from their mother. Only if their mother learns that they have done something "wrong," is it actually "wrong." These people take their mother seriously, but they do not take the idea "wrong" seriously. Consequently, only by assuming the idea "wrong" came from God would we take "wrong" seriously.

Conclusion: Therefore, God is alive in everyone's mind. Therefore, all persons, many subconsciously, assume God exists and they all behave as if they believe He exists because of their seriously taken perceptions of "wrong." Moreover, because God is a prerequisite in order for us to take our perceptions of "wrong" seriously, these seriously taken perceptions are indirectly perceptions of God Himself!

Corollary: Either evolution wrote God's existence into everyone's mind or God Himself did it. Our perceptions of right and wrong, and, therefore, God, are just as strong as our other perceptions. We take them just as seriously. We have complete faith in the other 99% of our perceptions to accurately reveal what exists. As a result, it would be unreasonable not to have faith in the last one per cent of our perceptions simply because they produce facts that demand morality. However, the vast majority of people, including little children, do have faith in their perceptions of "wrong" to reveal reality, which is confirmed by their belief in God. Because our seriously taken perceptions of "wrong" tell us God exists, belief in God is predominant throughout the entire world while atheism is the exception.

Every scientific fact depends on the trust, or faith, that our perceptions are accurate. Likewise, faith in our perceptions of "wrong" to accurately reveal what exists produces the scientific probability: God exists. Yes, God's

9

existence would be a scientific probability because of our justifiable faith in our seriously taken perceptions of "wrong."

If we take the step of faith to trust our sense of "wrong," exactly as we trust our other senses, to accurately reveal what exists, then we will discover the existence of the "God who demands morality." Discovering God will *always* need a step of faith, but it is exactly the same step of faith we take automatically, thousands of times every day, when we trust our other senses. It is also the same step of faith we need to take in order to discover *every* scientific fact!

Nevertheless, we are free to deny that God actually exists because it is possible that an outlandish quirk of evolution wrote God's existence into everyone's mind. Moreover, it is also possible that all our perceptions are illusions.

If our perceptions of "wrong" happen to be illusions, then God's existence would not have the foundation everyone's faith in their perceptions now give it. We are free to deny that God exists, because of the unlikely possibility "wrong" could be an illusion. All the same, our *faith* in our sense of "wrong," which gives us indirect perceptions of God, would still make His existence probable and perhaps a scientific certainty.

Think it over, because when people honestly examine why they take "wrong" so seriously, they usually acknowledge God's existence.

DEEPER ARGUMENTS

Millions of people and even little children believe that they know[3] God exists. Do you think that not one of the millions who believe in God has done so through sound moral

[3]Albert Einstein and Carl Seelig, *Ideas and Opinions* (New York: Crown Publishing Group, 1995) 18-24, 36-53. Using some of Einstein's ideas I define "know" as having achieved a true certainty through deductive reasoning or faith. (See footnote 2)

reasoning? Of course, many believers have used reason[4] to achieve their certainty that God exists; they just have never before verbalized that reasoning. The following essays verbalize exactly the reasoning they have used to achieve their certainty that God exists.

In verbalizing that reasoning, these essays encounter three major obstacles: First, they require some deep thought in order to understand this argument is a checkmate. They address every philosophical objection to this argument, which has made these essays a little more complicated than I would have liked. Second, a triumphant argument for God's existence is beyond the imagination of those who have allowed their environment to program their mind. Third, these essays employ reason, the intolerant and hated "thought policeman" who is constantly trying to destroy one of the world's most cherished freedoms: the freedom to believe to be true whatever a person wishes to be true.

These essays are an accurate, detailed and scientific explanation of the phenomenon: belief in God. In the manner of C.S. Lewis, they are based on certainties achieved by observing human behavior. Using these certainties it establishes the ultimate concept of moral arguments: A perception[5] of a seriously taken principle of objective morality is indirectly a perception of God Himself! These essays go on

---

[4]Ayn Rand, *Introduction to Objectivist Epistemology* (New York: Plume; Second Edition, Expanded Edition, 1990) 40-54. Also derived largely from Rand's definitions, I define "reason" as the mental process of adding facts to our mind's picture of what exists.

[5] I define "perception" as instinct, an inborn idea or anything our senses gather prior to reasoning. Wrongness is a perception. The shapes and colors we see are also perceptions; while "tree," formed after reasoning, is a concept. Further, I use the word "idea" to designate a perception or a concept.

to describe the exact process used by reasonable people to achieve the certainty that God exists. These essays' arguments, however, do not try to prove objectively that God exists. Yet, they establish that we have perceptions of God and that these perceptions produce the scientific probability: God exists. They do this through their advanced command of the implications of our behavior and the revelation that, outside mathematics, every scientific fact depends on a step of faith.

SCIENCE AND GOD

Many seem to be surprised at the philosophy of science. Science is not all-powerful. Some Postmodernist philosophers even say science does not have a foundation. They say this because every scientific fact is derived from what our senses tell us and it is *not* a logical necessity for our senses to be telling us the truth. We simply trust, or have faith, that our senses reveal to us what actually exists. Since everyone's faith in his or her senses is so automatic and so all-inclusive, we all initially have trouble grasping even the possibility that our senses could be deceiving us.

In order to establish God's existence as a scientific fact, we need to understand the foundation of scientific facts, which, outside mathematics, is *faith*. All scientific facts depend on faith in "naïve realism," faith in inductive reasoning or faith in the "uniformity of nature" (the Laws of Physics). Yes, every Law of Physics depends on a step of faith!

First, some scientific facts depend on faith in naïve realism. That is, these facts depend on our faith that the perceptions in our minds taken from our senses accurately reveal what actually exists. A scientific fact derived from what we see, for example, is based on our faith that the perceptions we get from our eyes accurately reveal what actually exists.

Second, the Laws of Physics depend on our faith that they will continue to be valid. It is not a logical necessity, for example, for a bouncing ball to continue to bounce according to the Law of Gravity. Scientists know exactly how a ball will bounce, but they do not know why it continues to bounce. They do not know why the uniformity of nature continues to be valid. Again, it is not a logical necessity for the Laws of Physics to continue to be valid. We all simply take a step of faith and assume that the Laws of Physics will be valid in the next five minutes as they are right now.

Third, we all have faith that inductive reasoning has provided us with scientific facts, in spite of the "problem of induction." The problem of induction is this: No matter how many times a scientific experiment gives the same result, it is not a logical necessity that the next result will be the same. We just have faith that the next result will be the same. Therefore, every scientific fact we have obtained through scientific experiments depends on a step of faith.

Some philosophers contend the problem of induction has no solution and, as a result, science is lame. Einstein indicated a solution for the problem of induction when he suggested that science is only lame without God. Einstein also suggested that the incomprehensible thing about science is that it is comprehensible. His suggestions strongly indicate that he thought it incomprehensible that science does not have a foundation and incomprehensible that the problem of induction and the problem of the uniformity of nature are not correctly solved by faith in a God who orders our world for our benefit. Consequently, as Einstein has helped to point out, it is incomprehensible that science would not have as its foundation the only foundation it could possibly have—faith in a loving God. And paraphrasing Bertrand Russell: If science does not have "faith in a loving God" as its foundation then there is no intellectual difference between sanity and insanity!

ON OBJECTIVE MORALITY

In my usage, I define objective morality as moral principles having three attributes: First, these principles transcend human opinion. Second, they are supremely authoritative; all of humanity is obligated to follow them. And third, they are not an exact moral code; reason establishes morality's principles for each situation.

C. S. Lewis referred to objective morality as the Real Morality. It has also been variously referred to as: the Law of Human Nature, Right and Wrong, the Voice of Reason and the Law of Love. While objective morality coincides with the human conscience or the human moral code, it can also be identified with the voice of Jesus, the commandments written in our hearts and the inborn inner pressure to understand and do what is right. In this essay, I use the terms "objective morality" and "objective moral principles" interchangeably with "right" and "wrong."

C. S. Lewis makes an important observation indicating that objective morality is a universal perception:

> "The moment you say that one set of moral ideas can be better than another, you are, in fact, measuring them both by a standard, saying that one of them conforms to that standard more nearly than the other. But the standard that measures two things is something different from either. You are in fact comparing them both with some Real Morality, admitting that there is such a thing as a real Right, independent of what people think and that some people's idea gets nearer to that of real Right than others."[6]

In his comment, Lewis establishes that everyone who promotes any idea of morality has an objective morality written into his or her mind.

_____

[6]C. S. Lewis, *Mere Christianity*, (New York: Harper Collins Publishers, 2001) 13.

Objective morality is not negated by moral diversity. It is of no consequence that everyone's idea of the principles of objective morality contradicts almost everyone else's. Most grasp the perceptions of objective morality written into their mind but many then add crooked thinking to those perceptions. Just as reason is needed to eliminate wrong answers and find the inherent answer to 1+2+3+1+4+2=, reason is also needed to eliminate moral diversity and discover objective morality.

Court cases are examples of the use of reason to discover objective morality. Moral truth in a court case is not a human convention; it exists to be discovered. When a court applies reason, by adding all the relevant facts together, it discovers objective morality. Suppose a person is being tried for murder. Reason is needed to determine whether he killed at all, killed in self-defense or committed murder. The court reaches the correct verdict if it uses reason to eliminate this moral diversity. This example reveals that perceptions of objective morality are inborn but the relevant facts for each situation are not. Objective morality would formally be described as a "synthetic *a priori* judgment."

The principles of objective morality have an interdependent relationship with reason. Reason discovers these principles while these principles, in turn, give reason the valuation of "right." Even though rationalizations can justify everything we do and justify everything we want, objective morality instead gives the valuation of "right" to reason. Reason is also evidence that objective moral principles are inborn. Since reason is universally recognized as "right," the idea "reason is right" is clearly inborn rather than learned.

C. S. Lewis makes the point that moral principles are still able to transcend human opinion even though teachers and parents teach them. He points out that teachers also teach the multiplication table, but it obviously transcends human opinion: "It [the multiplication table] is not something we made up and might have made different if we liked."[7]

In conclusion, an objective morality exists and this objective morality has been written into everyone's mind.

EUTHYPHRO'S DILEMMA

Euthyphro's Dilemma really does not have much to do with my argument for God's existence. My argument is purely propositional logic with a step of faith. It is: if such and such is true and we take a step of faith, then God's existence is a scientific certainty.

I have included this essay because some people claim that I need to address this important objection to God's existence. However, I suspect it may merely be a clever riddle, which is easily solved through "knowing thyself." Nevertheless, in deference to their urging I have added an analysis of this dilemma.

Euthyphro's Dilemma, from the *Dialogues of Plato*, has been used by some philosophers to claim that a God who commands us cannot possibly exist. They claim that either God's commands are a moral code He must abide by, making morality independent of Him; or, they claim that whatever God commands would be arbitrarily right, even if He commanded something evil. They conclude that either horn of this dilemma would disprove the existence of God.

The applicable version of this dilemma asks: "Does God command an act because it is good, or is an act good because it is commanded by God?" This dilemma is not "A or not A" rather it is "A or B" thereby leaving room for other options. The Bible creates another option by implying that an act can *never* be inherently good. No act inherently has the quality "good" (or in this case, "obedient") but it may acquire that quality just as an object may acquire the quality "carried." If a man, for example, commanded a servant to feed his cattle but

---

7 C.S. Lewis, *Mere Christianity* 12.

instead that servant plowed a field, then that act was not "good" or "obedient" even though it could possibly have those qualities at another time. In the same manner, when God commands an act, the act itself is not good. It is "obedience" that is good, which is not external of God. Therefore, addressing the first horn of this dilemma, no external moral code exists that the Biblical God needs to abide by.

Additionally, because God is love, the analogy that applies to Him is that of a father rather than a lawgiver. A father is not *bound* to command a beneficial act, but he does so because of love. Many earthly fathers have never commanded their children to do anything hurtful. They were not bound to act in this manner but they did so because they loved their children. Correspondingly, the Biblical God is not bound to command only beneficial acts but since He is good, He does command only beneficial acts.

The Bible declares only God's Nature is good[8] and only obedience to God is righteousness (piety). The piety that Socrates was looking for in this dialogue is Biblically known as obedience. Biblically speaking, obedience to God's command gives righteousness.

Next, some background about the second horn of this dilemma: would God be right if He commanded evil?

Would we still consider mass murder horrific if God did not exist? Perhaps not. Without God, our innate perception "mass murder is horrific" would need to come from another source. If it came from evolution or if we were all born with a blank mind, nothing would be stopping us from having the concept "mass murder is a necessity for survival" programmed into our minds. We then might become like certain apes that

---

[8] Philippians 2:13—For it is God who works in you both to will and to do of His good pleasure. (KJV) II Corinthians 4:7—But we have this treasure (the Holy Spirit) in earthen vessels, that the excellency of the power may be of God, and not of ourselves. (KJV)

routinely kill the offspring of rival apes to further the survival of their own offspring.

The idea "murder is wrong" is so overwhelming that most of us cannot even imagine something else written into our minds. Nevertheless, if the Biblical God had written into our minds "murder is right" we would esteem murder to be right just as the aforementioned apes do. If the Biblical God had commanded us to murder, we would have no innate ideas in our mind telling us murder is wrong. If God commanded us to murder, we would not doubt "murder is right" just as we now do not doubt "murder is wrong." Hence, whatever God commands would be right.

If God were mean-spirited, He could have commanded murder and pain to be right. Fortunately for us, the Biblical God is love. He wants for us our greatest long-term joy. Therefore, He wrote into our minds, "murder is wrong."

If God exists, nothing else would exist except Him and His creation. We could only attempt to judge God by the values He wrote into our mind. If God had written different values and ideas into our mind, as He did to Pharaoh in Exodus 9:12, our attempts to judge Him would be by those values and ideas. No matter what values we would use, our attempts to judge God would be ridiculous vanities! No moral code exists, no values exist, nothing exists outside of God to judge Him to be evil. God is right, even though He commanded the aforementioned apes to murder. Further, He is arbitrarily right, as in the Garden of Eden: You may eat this fruit but not that fruit. God is worthy to be praised because He could command something that caused unnecessary pain for us, which He does not do, and He would still be right.

Accordingly, the solution to Euthyphro's Dilemma is that while no moral code exists separately from God, whatever God arbitrarily commands is right, no matter how we happen to judge His commands. Think about it: A "God who commands us" is a contradiction and cannot possibly exist?! Obviously,

18

Euthyphro's Dilemma is merely a clever riddle perpetuated by those who do not know themselves.

RANDOM OBSERVATIONS

Moralities, such as Aristotle's virtues, J. S. Mill's utilitarianism, and different religious moralities are of no relevance to this argument because their existence does not negate the existence of an objective morality. This argument is not concerned with subjective moralities or whether some moralities partly coincide with the principles of objective morality. It is only concerned with establishing the fact that our perceptions of universal objective moral principles produce a scientific probability: God exists.

The "God Gene Theory," which states that only some people have a God gene, is irrelevant as well. If this essay reveals objective morality to be universal and that everyone has God's existence written into his or her mind, then everyone would have the God gene. This would make the God Gene Theory meaningless as a predictor of who would believe in God.

Evil is no problem for the Biblical God. Evil (deviations from an objective morality or sins or wrong) cannot possibly exist unless God exists! Who decrees what is evil? Evolution? Our parents? A religion? Only God has the authority to decree an action to be evil. (See the following "A Superior Argument.")

Why is there so much suffering in the world? Humanity is a long way from a beautiful, reasonable existence. Most people cannot imagine a beautiful, reasonable world with everyone in harmony. What these people call "horrific evils" could be necessities to prod humanity to make advances toward the millennium, that future beautiful existence.[9] Those

---

[9] Matthew 18:7a—Woe unto the world because of offenses! For it *needs* to be that offenses come. (KJV) Acts 14:22b—We must

who cannot imagine the millennium or imagine that God wrote every one of their innate values and every one of their judgments into their mind, will probably never be satisfied with any answer to the idea of suffering. They will simply never accept the big picture as Joseph did when he told his brothers, "You meant it for evil but God meant it for good." (Genesis 50:20) For myself, when I hear of suffering I become more determined to try to make the world a better place.

Furthermore, the Biblical God does not want His children to remain weak, ignorant, or faithless. For this reason, He gives us trials (evil, to some) in order to make us smarter and stronger. Similarly, He does not care for fair-weather followers. As a result, the Kingdom of God is something we are initiated into, which makes tribulation and persecution (evil) necessities.

A SUPERIOR ARGUMENT

The following argument is based on universally observed behavior. It takes place on the percept level of our minds, which postpones the question of whether or not God exists and makes it easier to answer this question later. This is an unusual version of an argument for God because it does not conclude: God exists. Instead, it concludes that God exists in everyone's mind. This conclusion is an accurate identification of what we know about God's existence while admitting what we do not know.

Premise 1: If God did not exist in our minds, then in our minds everything would be permitted.

Premise 2: However, in our minds some things are not permitted, such as most lying or most murders.

Conclusion: Therefore, in our minds, God exists.[10]

through much tribulation enter into the Kingdom of God. (KJV) II Timothy 3:12a—Yea, and all they who will live godly in Christ Jesus shall suffer persecution. (KJV)

Corollary: Either God Himself wrote into our minds the existence of a God who does not permit some things thereby obligating us to objective morality, or another source has done it.

EXPLANATIONS FOR THE PREMISES

Premise 1: If God did not exist in our minds, then in our minds everything would be permitted. If God did not exist, no action would be morally prohibited because God is the only legitimate moral authority. Governments have the authority to declare an action legally prohibited but not morally prohibited. Governments, for example, are unable to legislate against most lying. People, including you, are too emotional and too biased to authoritatively declare anything morally prohibited. Although reason discovers objective morality, it does not by itself determine objective morality. It is strictly the mental process of adding facts to our mind's picture of what exists. Accordingly, it does not have the authority to morally prohibit anything either. If you say whatever is detrimental to society is morally prohibited, you are then merely giving a definition to "morally prohibited." In this case, we would still need God to decree what is detrimental to society.

Moreover, if God did not author our conscience, and it evolved because of our hunter-gatherer past, then its directives would be outdated as well as subject to change at any time. An evolved conscience also would not have the authority to prohibit anything morally.

---

[10] This is a valid argument. The Conclusion logically follows from Premise 1 and Premise 2. Propositional logic dictates that denying the consequent (everything is permitted) negates the antecedent (God does not exist). The soundness of an argument, however, depends on the truth of its premises.

21

If God authored our conscience, then it is an extension of Himself. Having eliminated the other plausible candidates, He then, through our conscience, would be the only legitimate authority for declaring actions morally prohibited. Considering that God is the only legitimate moral authority, everything would be permissible if we did not believe (consciously or subconsciously) He authored objective morality. On top of that, by virtue of being the only authority who could enforce objective morality, if we did not believe God enforced objective morality, then in our minds everything would be permitted.

Premise 2: However, in our minds some things are not permitted, such as most lying or most murders. We all consider some form of lying or murder not permitted. Even more than that, children without any previous knowledge of or any previous experience with certain abuses, even though those abuses do not cause physical pain, consider those abuses not permitted because they are so devastating. This fact conclusively reveals the existence of inborn objective morality, which does not permit some things.

Conclusion: Therefore God exists in our minds. If perceptions of things not permitted and, as a result, perceptions of seriously taken principles of objective morality exist in our minds, then perceptions of God exist in our minds. These are perceptions of God because our perceptions of objective morality include the idea "serious." The idea "serious" cannot be included in our perceptions of objective morality without being preceded by perceptions of God's authority *and* by perceptions of God's enforcement. If our perceptions of objective morality included the idea "absurd," or "bothersome," or even "appropriate for humanity" without the idea "serious" then they would translate to perceptions from evolution or from a human source rather than from God. However, everyone has at least one perception of objective morality that includes the idea "serious." Therefore, everyone has God's existence written into his or her mind.

Incidentally, crooked thinking, cultural deformations or a completely fabricated sense of "wrong" does not prohibit us from having perceptions of God. However, if they were added to our perceptions of God they would distort or falsify our concept of God.

Corollary: Either God Himself wrote into our minds the existence of a God who does not permit some things thereby obligating us to objective morality, or another source has done it. Many explanations are possible for the existence of a God in our minds besides evolution and God. Repetitions of rationalizations, religious teachings or even space aliens could be responsible for our belief in God. However, the existence of a God who obligates us to objective morality could only plausibly have been written into our minds by either evolution, because it transcends human opinion, or by God Himself, just as the Biblical God promises to do in Hebrews 10:16.

Even though we all have God's existence written into our minds, it is conceivable that evolution wrote it there. Either an outlandish quirk of evolution wrote the existence of a "God who demands morality" into everyone's mind or God Himself has done it. As a result, God has given us the option to deny Him, even if that option is extremely unreasonable.

Every creature on earth has faith! From the bugs that crawl, to the birds that fly, to the fish that swim in the sea, every creature has complete faith in every one of its perceptions to accurately reveal what exists. Furthermore, without this faith they could not survive. Are humans the only living creatures who do not need faith in their every perception to survive? What do you think?

THE RATIONAL CERTAINTY GOD EXISTS

Millions of people know God exists because they have achieved that certainty by adding these facts, *usually subconsciously*, to their mind's picture of what exists: First, they have added the fact that they have taken a step of faith to believe in naïve realism. That is, they trust that the perceptions in their mind taken from their senses accurately reveal what actually exists. Second, they have added the fact that they have taken a step of faith to believe in inductive reasoning. That is, they trust that a certain collection of previous experiences will predict future experiences. Third, they have added the fact that they have taken a step of faith to believe in the uniformity of nature. That is they trust, for example, that a bouncing ball will continue to bounce according to the Law of Gravity when it is not a logical necessity for it to do so. Fourth, they have added the fact that all these steps of faith produce what is universally accepted as true knowledge. Fifth, they have added the fact that their perceptions of the principles of objective morality ("wrong") contain the idea "serious," which give them (indirect) perceptions of God. And sixth, they have taken the step of faith to accept that their perceptions of God are true knowledge also.

In other words, these believers know God exists because their perceptions of God give them the same degree of certainty as they have when they know they see a tree. Second, they know God exists because their perceptions of God give them the same degree of certainty as they have when they know eating a slice of bread will nourish them. And third, they know God exists because their perceptions of God give them the same degree of certainty as they have when they know the next time they drop a ball it will bounce according to the Law of Gravity.

Because of these facts, the step from having perceptions of God written into our minds to discovering God exists is not a big step at all. We would be completely inconsistent with every aspect of our existence if we did not take this reasonable step of faith and accept the fact that the God who has been written into our minds does indeed exist. If our perceptions of "wrong" are correct, as everyone assumes, then God exists.

SYNOPSIS

Those who use pompous language and overly complicated arguments and convoluted counter-arguments cannot possibly be discussing the Biblical God. He claims that His existence and His commands are manifestly obvious to everyone—even to little children.

C. S. Lewis seems to be one of the few modern thinkers who wrote clearly and simply about God's existence. Others, however, have made important advances. Richard Swinburne contends that there is no "great probability that moral awareness will occur in a Godless universe."[11] He came close to discovering this argument, however, he stopped just short of asking, Why do we take moral awareness seriously? Robert M. Adams argues that our moral obligation is identical to God's command, but misses the clearer Biblical concept of the voice of Jesus, which happens to be spiritually identical to our conscience. He also argues that a "great good" comes from a relationship with God, but falls just short of stating that this "great good" is spiritual joy now and forever. Adams does an exemplary job escaping *Euthyphro's Dilemma* by arguing for God's goodness, however he could clarify his argument a bit by using the Biblical concept: God is our Father.[12]

In spite of their great scholarship, these philosophers lack the self-knowledge to understand that God's commands are both loving and arbitrary. They also analyze the idea of moral awareness while omitting the deeper idea of moral seriousness. So of course, they miss the concept that we cannot take our sense of "wrong" seriously without presupposing God. They also seem to accept J. S. Mill's false assertion that the moral laws in our mind could not have a

---

[11]Swinburne, R., 2004, *The Existence of God*, 2nd edition, Oxford: Oxford University Press.
[12]Adams, R., 1987, *The Virtue of Faith and Other Essays in Philosophical Theology*, New York: Oxford University Press, 144-163.

legislator. In addition, their writings seem to be oblivious to faith as a philosophical idea. We need faith not only to discover God but also to discover science! None of their writings shows a command of much needed Biblical concepts, such as: God is within us; God wrote our innate ideas into our minds; and spiritual joy is our pathfinder for what we ought to do and therefore defines our obligation to God.

My arguments have attempted to substantiate these two statements: (1) Our seriously taken perceptions of "wrong" give us perceptions of God. And (2) our perceptions produce scientific certainties. I believe these arguments succeed. Therefore, I believe that anyone can "know" (see footnotes 2 and 3) God exists and that it is a scientific probability, and perhaps even a scientific fact, that He exists.

Some, however, may say that they doubt the origins or even the existence of our perceptions of "wrong." I will not compel them to trust or distrust their perceptions. Again, discovering God's existence will always require the step of faith that our perceptions of "wrong" accurately reveal what exists: God. Sad to say, many refuse to take that step of faith.

Again, it is highly probable that the Biblical God wrote "right" and "wrong" into our minds. These moral principles in our minds and the Biblical commandments are similar, if not identical. The Biblical God demands the objective moral principle of "reason" for both salvation (Isaiah 1:18) and faith (Luke 12:24). The Bible also uses the universal word "conscience" more than twenty times when describing its morality. In another similarity with objective morality, Biblical morality demands mercy instead of religious rules.

Unreasonable people have muddied the waters for centuries. Do not allow them to confuse you; the argument about God's existence is not a stalemate. Reason is squarely on God's side. He created reason, which discovers everything in His creation and now discovers God Himself as well.

The Biblical God may even use reason to fulfill His promise to convince the unreasonable of their deviations from the principles of objective morality (sins). For no other process besides reason exists to correctly convince anyone of anything.

God may compel them to admit the fact they had always known His commands were written into their mind because it would be unfair for Him to condemn a person if that person did not know His commands beforehand. Until that day, unfortunately, many will continue their rationalizations, their crooked thinking, and their frivolous denials of God. They could escape a bad end if only they could take to heart the ancient Greek directive: Know thyself.[13]

However, you and I, and even little children have always known God exists; and now reason supports that certainty. Of course, the God who obligates us to objective morality, the God who wrote the Law of Love in our hearts does indeed exist. Moreover, He plainly reveals that He exists. Praise Him for that!

---

[13] The Biblical God is not bound by objective morality because the Bible says He overrules it to show us mercy. Psalms 86:5— For you, Lord, are good, and ready to forgive; plenteous in mercy unto all them that call unto you. (KJV) Isaiah 55:7—Let the wicked forsake his way, and the unrighteous man his thoughts: and let him return unto the LORD and He will have mercy upon him. (KJV) The origin of the directive, know thyself, is usually attributed to an inscription on the ancient Temple of Apollo at Delphi, Greece.

SECTION II -
ESSAYS FROM CHRISTIAN
OBJECTIVISM'S "THEOLOGY OF
EXTREME JOY"

Leaping for joy *because* someone lied about you? Now that is extreme! (Luke 6:22, 23) However, is it idiotic to do that or is it profoundly wise?

CHRISTIAN OBJECTIVISM

I call my theology Christian Objectivism because it is based on God's administration of reason and on two of reason's interdependent relationships. The first is reason's relationship with faith. Reason is grounded in faith in a loving God while faith in God is built by reason. The second is reason's relationship with the human conscience. Reason discovers the directives of the conscience while the conscience, in turn, gives reason the valuation of good. Christian Objectivism is so complete it only needs one directive: be reasonable. Everything we need to know and everything we need to do can be completely understood by sound reasoning, which is defined as the adding to our mind's picture the true certainties we have achieved through our experiences. This is the definition of reason that God Himself uses in Isaiah 1:18. Above all, the directives of our conscience are the most important of these certainties.

I (Christian Objectivism) hold the process of reason (inductive) to be the basis of human knowledge, just as Ayn Rand's Objectivism does, but I do not hold reason supreme. I hold supreme the Biblical God who requires reason for every successful endeavor. In addition, correctly solving the problem of induction, Christian Objectivism understands that reason is grounded in the faith that the loving Biblical God will continue reason's validity. Otherwise, there would be no possible solution for the problem of induction, and no possible foundation for our certainties!

The problem of induction is this: No matter how many times a scientific experiment gives the same result, there is still no proof that the next result will be the same. We just have faith that the next result will be the same. Therefore, the only foundation science and reason can possibly have is faith.

Christian Objectivism is superior to Objectivism because it has a foundation for "reason." It is also a more accurate identification of reality because it adds the human conscience to our minds' picture of what exists. On top of that, since Christian Objectivism has the most reasonable picture of reality, its application brings the greatest joy.

The transcendent natures of Christian Objectivism's reason and the human conscience have even been observed independently of Christianity and western civilization. Nakaye Toju of the Japanese Oyomei School of Philosophy in the early 17th century wrote, "If we act in accord with reason or conscience, we are ourselves the incarnations of the infinite and eternal, and have eternal life."[14]

REASON

You may have been surprised by how much this book promotes reasonableness. However, the more reasonable we are, the more unified we are with Jesus and God. God administers His universe entirely through reason. Our Father in heaven is reasonable about everything, including salvation and faith. If we are reasonable, then He will reveal to us many spiritual treasures.

Inductive reasoning is simply the process of adding facts to our mind's picture of what exists. A fact is a certainty

[14]*The Story of Civilization*, Will and Ariel Durant, (New York, Simon and Schuster, 1935) Vol. 1, 871.

achieved through generalizations of previous experiences. Experiences also determine whether a generalization is a false hasty generalization or a true certainty.

Reason has four major enemies: emotionalism, religious superstitions, fear, and principles. Emotionalism is characterized by: I want this, I want that, and I want more. Emotional people think if they submit to reason, they might not get everything they want. Religious superstitions are traditions that some blindly follow because they are deceived by them. Some, for example, believe God wants them to perform unreasonable ritual prayers. Fear causes some to say and do what others want instead of being reasonable and honest. However, "principles" could be the most subtle enemy of reason. Acting in accordance with the same principle in every situation thoughtlessly prohibits reasoned actions that benefit everyone.

Reason correctly solves every dispute and argument. When the facts each person presents are added together, the complete picture of the dispute can be seen and the correct solution realized. Reason has never failed. It is only the human mind that sometimes fails in its ability to discover and add facts together.

Reason is often counterfeited by sophisticated rationalizations. We are bombarded with dozens of these rationalizations every day, which we often mistake for sound reasoning. I have heard, for example, this rationalization: 'We are saved by hope; I hope I am saved; therefore I must be saved.' This rationalization confuses the act of "hoping in Jesus" with the act of "hoping for salvation." Can you imagine God honoring a rationalization like this one? Of course, God will not honor it. He is reasonable and only honors sound moral reasoning.

God even uses the process of reason for salvation. In Isaiah 1:18, God says, "Come now, let us reason together though your sins be as scarlet they shall be white as snow." God is saying that He will consider any fact we want to bring to

Him and that He wants us to accept the fact we are sinners. Only then can our contract for eternal life can be finalized. The Bible requires reason for our eternal survival just as our physical survival requires reason. However, some people are too ignorant of their own character or too weak to add the relevant facts to their minds' picture. They just use rationalizations or fabricated doctrines, instead of reason, to build their relationship with God.

Biblical faith is also developed through reason. The Bible says that if we consider (add to our minds' picture) the fact God takes care of the flowers and the animals, we will grow in faith (Luke 12:24). The Bible also teaches in Hebrews 11 that the more experiences with God we have, the more faith we will have in Him. The more we ask God to help us, the more we will trust Him. Having faith in God can be described as achieving certainties about God through reading His Word and through our experiences with the Law of Love that He wrote in our heart.

Faith in God does not contradict reason because true faith in God adds every relevant fact together. The faiths that contradict reason are faith in religious absurdities and faith in fabrications that someone has programmed into our mind. These faiths omit essential facts and usually contain rationalizations as well. Faith in these human fabrications is a killjoy. Those who have no faith in what God wrote in their heart are unreasonable killjoys and infidels. Faith in the Biblical God and in His Word is good because it brings spiritual joy.

That we may be delivered from *unreasonable* and wicked men: for all men have not faith. -II Thessalonians 3:2

THE HUMAN CONSCIENCE

All animals are given within their instinct the required knowledge for surviving in this world. All animals, that is, except humans. We have been given a desire to survive in this world but we must learn how to do so. However, we have been given an instinct that gives us the required knowledge for surviving in the next world. This inborn instinct is our conscience, which is another term for the voice of Jesus or the laws God wrote in our heart.

Is our conscience an absurdity because it gives directives for survival in the next world? No, we are the only animals who know long beforehand that we will die, so we are the only ones who would need an instinct for survival in the next world. Is the conscience an absurdity because it gives directives with no enforcer of those directives? Of course, our conscience is not an absurdity, so an enforcer of its directives must exist—God. If God does not exist, the conscience, which demands reasonableness, would itself be an unreasonable absurdity. If we esteem the conscience as an authority, then we are assuming God will enforce its directives.

Did God create our conscience or did our conscience fabricate God? Those who hate the demands their conscience makes on them say that God is a fabrication. However, could the conscience, which prohibits lying, itself be a lie? Those who deny God and their conscience are speaking lies in hypocrisy having their conscience seared as with a hot iron. (I Timothy 4:2)

The fool has said in his heart, There is no God. —Psalm. 14:1

Our conscience is our fountainhead of spiritual joy, our bond with humanity and our link to God (Acts 24:16). It is our God-given instinct for survival, in this case eternal survival. However, the forces of evil are always trying to convince us that our conscience is meaningless. The entertainment industry presents a stylized reality that completely omits the conscience. Many psychoanalysts say the conscience is merely a set of taboos copied from parents or society. In addition, religious leaders say their rules are sacred—not the directives God wrote in our conscience. Even with all these evils raging against the conscience, it still triumphs because of the tremendous joy and satisfaction God gives us every time we obey His directives written in our conscience. And one moment of this joy outweighs the thousands of lies denying the conscience!

The directives in our conscience concern how we treat others; they explain what love is. The first directive of our conscience is: be reasonable. As I have pointed out, we need reason for salvation and faith but reason is also an important part of love. Those under an authority always want those who have worldly power to submit to this directive. Citizens want those who govern them to be reasonable; workers want their employer to be reasonable; and children want their parents to be reasonable. Being reasonable is one of the most important parts of our conscience's revelation of love.

Most are not aware of the danger of eroding their conscience. If a person erodes his conscience to the point it is completely erased, he permanently ends his own existence. No one can destroy another's conscience and the only conscience a person can destroy is his own. Therefore, no one can kill another person permanently; the only person anyone can actually kill permanently is himself.

The human conscience is fragile. Just ignoring it can erode it and destroy it. Those who commit horrible criminal acts reveal that they have destroyed their conscience and no longer have the quality of humanness. Those who destroy their conscience also dedicate themselves to self-deception. Worse yet, many of them hate those who still have a conscience. They often impudently say to those who follow their conscience, "Oh, you are so virtuous." This statement is an attempt to intimidate others into destroying their conscience just as they have done.

Even their mind and conscience is defiled. –Titus 1:15b

The Bible refers to those who have destroyed their conscience as goats. On the last day, God shall set the sheep on the right hand but the goats on the left (Matthew 25:33).

Here are five actions that can erode and destroy a person's conscience. However, if a conscience is merely eroded and not destroyed, it can be restored through prayer and sound moral reasoning.

Sex outside of marriage—Fornication is the number one activity that will erode our conscience. Some have said, "The first time I fornicated I felt guilty, but now I don't feel guilty at all." These people may have committed spiritual suicide. Their comment reveals their conscience is now badly eroded or worse.

Say unto wisdom, You are my sister; and call understanding your kinswoman: that they may keep you from the strange woman, from the stranger which flatters with her words. For at the window of my house, I looked through my casement and beheld among the simple ones, I discerned among the youths, a young man void of understanding, passing through the street near her corner; and he went the way to her house, in the twilight, in the evening, in the black and dark night. And behold, there met him a woman with the attire of an harlot, and subtil of heart. (She is loud and stubborn; her feet abide not in her house. Now is she without, now in the streets, and lies in wait at every corner.) So she caught him, and kissed him, and with an impudent face said unto him, I have peace offerings with me; this day have I paid my vows. Therefore came I forth to meet you, diligently to seek your face, and I have found thee. I have decked my bed with coverings of tapestry, with carved works, with fine linen of Egypt. I have perfumed my bed with myrrh, aloes, and cinnamon. Come, let us take our fill of love until the morning: let us solace ourselves with loves. For the good man is not at home; he is gone on a long journey. He has taken a bag of money with him, and will come home at the day appointed. With her much fair speech she caused him to yield, with the flattering of her lips she forced him. He went after her straightway, as an ox goes to the slaughter, or as a fool to the correction of the stocks; till a dart strike through his liver; as a bird hastes to the snare, and knows not that it is for his life. Hearken unto me now therefore, O ye children, and attend to the words of my mouth. Let not your heart decline to her ways, go not astray in her paths. For she has cast down many wounded: yea, many strong men have been slain by her. Her house is the way to hell, going down to the chambers of death.–Proverbs 7:4-27

Again, God is full of mercy for all who call on Him (Psalm 86:5).

Lying—Lying to another person is a close second in eroding the conscience. People lie because it gives them an advantage over others in obtaining material possessions. Others lie because they are too weak to face the consequences of their actions. Some lie because they are afraid people will become angry if they tell the truth. Additionally, there are those who lie just for sport, not understanding that God judges our every word. If Jesus did not promise to burn all liars in a lake of fire, lying would be a smart thing to do. However, Jesus does promise that, and so lying is not smart but an ignorant thing to do.

And all liars shall have their part in the lake of fire, which is the second death. –Revelation 21:8

Hate—The motivations for hate are as varied as they are for lying. Some people hate because they want others to be as miserable as they are. Some overreact to being hated and destroy themselves by returning hate. Others hate because it is easier to blame someone else for their sins than to take responsibility for their own actions.

Stupefying yourself—Repeated intoxications will destroy your conscience. Usually, those who intoxicate themselves are unable to face the obstacles God has given them. They never achieve the strength, wisdom, and great joy that overcoming obstacles brings.

Becoming a religious proselyte—Religious proselytes are those who decide to destroy their conscience and replace it with a fabricated moral authority—religious rules.

They forsake the command to show mercy and replace it with their desire to condemn others for not following their self-chosen rules. Many become proselytes because of their great love for self-righteousness and for condemning others.

Loving rules instead of people makes a person a proselyte. We can *know* we are a child of God and not a proselyte if we rejoice in mercy rather than in religious rules.

Your conscience will bear witness to the Truth. –Romans 9:1

Now the end of the commandment is love from a pure heart and a good conscience.–I Timothy 1:5

For our rejoicing is this, the testimony of our conscience. –II Corinthians 1:12

THE BIBLE

If the Bible had a subtitle, it would be "How to Be Profoundly Happy, Now and Forever." Everything in the Bible has been written so that we can obtain eternal joy. Jesus said, in John 15:11 that the reason He was preaching was so that we could be eternally filled with joy. The Apostle John writes the same thing in I John 1:4. Likewise, the Apostle Paul writes, in II Corinthians 1:24 that his purpose is to be a helper of people's joy. These three said specifically they want believers to be filled with joy.

The supreme value in the Bible is spiritual joy. The Bible even esteems joy higher than love. Jesus commands us to love because when we love, God fills us with joy. Notice Jesus did not say, I have spoken these things so that you will be filled with love. He puts our joy first because He really does love us. God is love because His greatest desire is for us to be filled with spiritual joy. When we work for God, love is the work we do and joy is our payment. If we say we love God, that means we have been working diligently for Him feeding His sheep with understanding or doing acts of mercy. "Agape" love is not lip service or a warm fuzzy feeling—agape love is work.

36

Love is the highest virtue of the Bible, but our joy is its supreme value. Therefore, if we are walking in God's Spirit, our purpose for talking to people in Jesus' Name should be to help them be filled with spiritual joy. All too often, preaching in Jesus' Name is inspired by other motives.

The dominant doctrine of the Bible is mercy. All other doctrines, such as repentance and faith, are incorporated into mercy. When the "Good Samaritan" (Luke 10:30-37) showed mercy to the roadside victim he first needed to repent of whatever he had previously budgeted his money for and repent of his previous schedule. He also needed to have faith that mercy was what God wanted him to do in spite of his cultural traditions.

Do not let anyone deceive you about Biblical doctrine. Bible doctrine is: if we ask for mercy and show mercy, we will gain eternal life; if we do not show mercy, we will not obtain eternal life. A person's doctrine may be what some leader has programmed into his mind; it may be legalistic rules; it may be the lust for vainglory; or it may be mercy. There is no need to ask a person about his doctrine, just observe him. Everyone shall know if a person has the right doctrine of love and mercy merely by observing him (John 13:35). Either a person acts on a belief in mercy or he does not act on it.

Besides the parable of *The Good Samaritan*, three other parables reveal the importance of mercy. In the parable of *The Wicked Servant* (Matthew 18:23-35), this servant refused to show mercy even after he was granted mercy, so he was punished. In the parable of *The Rich Man and Lazarus* (Luke 16:19-31), the rich man is not accused of any sin. His only fault is not showing mercy to Lazarus. That was enough to condemn him to a lake of fire. In the parable of *The Goats and the Sheep* (Matthew 25:32-46), mercy is the only criterion used to decide whether a person will spend eternity in heaven or be cast into everlasting punishment.

Furthermore, Jesus gives us a lifetime assignment to learn about mercy. In Matthew 9:13 He says, "But go and learn what this means: I desire mercy and not sacrifice. For I have not come to call the righteous, but sinners to repentance." Nothing else in the Bible trumps the command to show mercy to our neighbor. Showing mercy is not a "dead works trip." It is essential for a joyous eternal life.

I would like to clarify our Biblical duty because many have been deceived into thinking God will tell them to do something distasteful. Our Biblical duty does not include following religious rules or senseless "musts." Our duty to God, in a roundabout way, is to experience spiritual joy. For we only obtain this joy by doing what God wants us to do. Spiritual joy is the payment He gives us when we have faith in His command to manifest His attributes. Love is our work; joy is our payment. Thus, spiritual joy is the highest Biblical value. Joy is our payment for love, faith, and other Biblical values as well as the pathfinder for what we *ought* to do. Biblical morality is opaquely recognized by the secular world as: When I do good I feel good; when I do bad I feel bad.

When we are not doing what God wants, He takes our joy away, as He did with King David, who felt very bad and prayed fervently for his joy to be restored.

Restore unto me the joy of thy salvation. -Psalm 51:12

Many say the Bible could not have survived thousands of years without being corrupted and that it contains many errors, if it is true at all. Regardless, we can test the Bible right now by applying its teachings to our life. If these teachings bring profound joy for you, as they have for me, then you can be certain the Bible is true. No one knows what happened throughout history first-hand, but everyone knows first-hand whether he or she is experiencing spiritual joy.

The Bible is correct in demanding reasonableness. It is correct in holding the human conscience (the voice of Jesus) as humankind's moral authority. It is correct in teaching that religious rules are humankind's greatest enemy. It is also correct in teaching that if we love others we will be filled with joy. The fact the Bible is correct, coinciding with our

38

conscience, in its major teachings inspires our trust that everything else in the Bible is correct also.

Even though the Bible was written thousands of years ago, it is more morally reasonable than any religion practiced today. It is the only religious entity that embraces reason. It is the only religious entity that condemns religious rules. It is the only religious entity that says our duty to God is to experience joy by following the laws our Creator wrote in our heart. An earthly influence could not have inspired a document more morally reasonable and more advanced than any earthly influence has ever been. The Bible could only have been inspired by our Creator.

GOD'S NEW CONTRACT FOR SALVATION

This is the covenant I will make with them after those days, saith the Lord, I will put my laws into their hearts, and in their minds will I write them. -Hebrews 10:16

I have been amazed at how few people understand God's New Covenant, even though it is plainly stated in the Bible. Knowing the Biblical contract for eternal life is *essential* for our confidence and our spiritual joy. God has established a new contract with humankind for our salvation. The laws of the Old Testament of the Bible established the old contract, but in the New Testament God has established a new and different covenant, or contract, for His people today. Everyone has heard repeatedly, in John 3:16, about God's side of this new contract. He completed His part of the new contract for our salvation when He sent Jesus to pay for our sins. Yet, few people have even heard of our obligation in this new contract.

Our obligation in God's New Covenant for salvation is to obey the Law of Love that God has written in our heart. Following the commandments in our heart is how we fulfill our part of the contract with God for the salvation of our soul. If we are not able to follow these commandments, God only requires us to be honest and ask for mercy. Remember, the

39

commandments in our heart are the standard God wants us to try to follow. This is essential information for everyone who wants to become immortal and experience an eternity of joy.

Salvation has nothing to do with church attendance, public prayer or dietary rules. Rather, it has everything to do with mercy and compassion. God did not write religious rules in our hearts, He wrote the *Law of Love* in our hearts.

Wherefore if you be dead with Christ from the rudiments of the world, why as though living in the world are you subject to ordinances, such as, touch not; taste not; and handle not. -Colossians 2:20

My sheep hear my voice, and I know them, and they follow me: And I give unto them eternal life; and they shall never perish, neither shall any man pluck them out of my hand.-John 10:27, 28

The people of God hear Jesus' voice. Every one of Jesus' sheep hears His voice. This does not involve mysticism or an out of control imagination; hearing His voice is a revelation of love from within our heart. Listening to Jesus' voice, which is within each one of us, is the only way to experience God's love revealed. If we do not listen to Jesus' voice, we can only make a bad guess as to what *agape* love is.

Once when I was teaching a Bible Study in the Philippines, a young girl asked me, "How do we know that the voice of Jesus is not just our imagination?" I told her, "Suppose you see someone drop a 5-peso coin. One voice will tell you to keep it and one voice will tell you to give it back. Which voice do you think is the voice of Jesus?" She answered correctly.

And he said, Go forth, and stand upon the mount before the Lord. And, behold, the Lord passed by, and a great and strong wind rent the mountains, and brake in pieces the rocks before the Lord; but the Lord was not in the wind: and after the wind an earthquake; but the Lord was not in the earthquake: And after the earthquake a fire; but the Lord was

not in the fire: and after the fire a *still small voice.*
-I Kings 19:11, 12

Beware of people who make false claims about hearing the voice of Jesus. The first thing Jesus teaches a person is how to love. How can it be that Jesus has told someone many things but never taught that person to love? Everyone shall recognize the followers of Jesus by the love they manifest (John 13:35).

Today if you hear God's voice, harden not your hearts; lest you be hardened through the deceitfulness of sin. -Hebrews 3:7b, 8, 13

The directive to not harden our hearts is one of the most important warnings in the Bible. When we first stray from the narrow path of love, we will feel guilty. (Do not confuse this with false feelings of guilt that arise from breaking the commandments of men.) If we continually and willfully sin, our feelings of guilt will disappear with the erosion of our conscience. This diminishes our ability to hear Jesus' voice explaining the path of love.

Many people trust in a covenant fabricated by men, thinking it is a valid covenant with God. Entering into a false contract of religious rules will not lead to eternal joy. Fabricating a false covenant with God that mixes religious rules with the law of love is what makes hypocrites dead in their sins. It only takes a little poison in an otherwise nourishing meal to ruin it. Likewise, it only takes one religious rule to ruin spiritual joy.

A friend of mine enjoyed playing basketball. He was even on a national team for a while. This changed when he married a woman who was a Saturday-keeper. In his heart, he knew playing basketball on Saturday was not wrong, but he obeyed his wife and stopped playing on that day. Just one religious rule made him a slave and hindered his joy.

A little leaven leavens the whole lump. –Galatians 5:9

By obeying the Law of Love written in our heart, we can achieve the invincible, true certainty that we have obtained

41

eternal life. We are assured of this certainty by the tremendous joy God gives us and because we know that we have not denied any relevant facts about salvation.

Many people have been deceived into making a false contract with God for salvation. Some false contracts include going to church, dietary rules, wearing absurd clothing, following rituals or saying memorized prayers. All these contracts, however, will be abruptly cancelled on Judgment Day. On that day, God will destroy every fortress of unreasonable ideas.

Because you have said, we have made a covenant with death and with hell we are at agreement, when the overflowing scourge shall pass through, it shall not come unto us for we have made lies our refuge and under falsehood have we hid ourselves. Therefore your covenant with death shall be disannulled and your agreement with hell shall not stand. -Isaiah 28:15, 18

THE MYSTERY

But we speak the wisdom of God in a mystery, even the hidden wisdom, which God ordained before the world unto our glory: which none of the princes of this world knew: for had they known it, they would not have crucified the Lord of glory. -I Corinthians 2:7, 8

One of the greatest revelations made by God was the revelation of the mystery to the Apostle Paul. It is certainly equal to, or greater than, the revelation of the Ten Commandments to Moses or the Revelation of Jesus Christ to the Apostle John. When Satan rebelled against God, he believed he could be victorious. However, God hid from him one aspect of His plan for man's salvation. God called His hidden plan for man's salvation, The Mystery. He later revealed this plan to the Apostle Paul.

Even the mystery which has been hid from ages and from generations, but is now made manifest to his saints: to whom

God would make known what is the riches of the glory of this mystery among the Gentiles; which is *Christ in you*, the hope of glory. -Colossians 1:26, 27

The mystery is this: Jesus lived perfectly, sacrificed His life on the cross and was resurrected. Because of this, His Spirit can now live within every child of God. This is something Satan never understood. Unfortunately, many believers do not realize this either. Children of God need to know that because Jesus' Spirit is alive within each one of us, we now have the same access to God's voice and God's power that Jesus had.

We will triumph over evil when we know and understand God's power within us. The voice of Jesus is alive within our hearts with the guidance, direction and teaching that our souls need. We do not need to teach Christ-in-us anything, we do not need to improve Him and we do not need to make Him appear better. When we comprehend the mystery, we will grasp the importance of manifesting Jesus' love from our hearts rather than trying to make our carnal nature seem Christ-like.

Some preachers, who do not understand manifesting Jesus from the heart, say people should attempt to be Christ-like. Yet, the most Christ-like being in the universe is Satan. A Christ-like life is a satanic life and a satanic life is a Christ-like life. Christ-like people make going to church their most important duty. However, when our hearts rejoice in mercy, we know that God has transformed us into His children. The fellowship of the mystery happens when Christ in us is fellowshipping with Christ in our neighbor. Paul wanted everyone to discover this fellowship because it brings great joy.

And to make all men see what is the fellowship of the mystery. -Ephesians 3:9

Because of the mystery, the fact Christ is in us, backsliding is never mentioned in the New Testament. Since Christ lives in us, we are not subject to rules or laws from which we could backslide. Anyone who talks of backsliding in today's world is ignorant of the doctrine of Christ. Instead, Jesus warns us not to cover the light within us, for it is still possible for us to manifest our carnal nature (Romans 7:21).

For it is not you that speak, but the spirit of your Father which speaks in you. -Matthew 10:20

Know you not your own selves, that Jesus Christ is in you, except you be reprobates? -II Corinthians 13:5

GOD'S RIGHTEOUSNESS

For I bear them record they have a zeal for God, but not according to knowledge. For they being ignorant of God's righteousness, and going about to establish their own righteousness, have not submitted themselves unto the righteousness of God. –Romans 10:2, 3

Herein is love, not that we loved God, but that He loved us while we were yet sinners. -I John 4:10

The ancient Romans needed to know the difference between their righteousness and God's righteousness. That knowledge is still needed today. God's righteousness is established by His love, not ours. God loves us unconditionally, in spite of the fact that we sin and not because of anything we do. We are all sinners; therefore, we all need to ask for forgiveness and mercy to obtain God's righteousness. We manifest God's righteousness only when we are in obedience to God. We do *not* establish God's righteousness by saying: See how much better I am now that I am a Christian. We establish God's righteousness by saying: See how good God is because He loves even me, a sinner!

Some people try to demonstrate that because they are a Christian they are good or a better person. These are attempts to establish their own righteousness, righteousness without God or self-righteousness. Our righteousness, which is self-righteousness, is manifested in many ways. Some say, "I go to church every Sunday," or, "I always pay my tithes," or, "I work

44

hard for everything I have." This kind of righteousness is similar to throwing trash at God.

All our righteousnesses are as filthy rags. -Isaiah 64:6

Christ is become of no effect to you if you are justified by the law; you are fallen from grace. Galatians 5:4

For by grace are you saved through faith; and that not of yourselves. It is the gift of God, not of works lest any man should boast. –Ephesians 2:8, 9

Following rules has nothing to do with loving our neighbor. All rules are fulfilled in one command—love your neighbor as yourself (Galatians 5:14). It is a tremendous joy to know: (1) we do not need to follow a set of rules for God to love us and (2) we need only show mercy to others for God to show us mercy. When we are devoted to our own righteousness, we are focused on ourselves in order to keep religious rules. This kills our joy. When we embrace God's righteousness, we are focused on others in order to show them mercy. This brings our deepest joy.

Making mistakes or committing sins does indeed ruin our testimony and our righteousness. However, we can now testify of God's goodness by proclaiming that God still loves us even though we do not deserve His love. This shows why God's grace is indeed amazing. Since our sins show the abundance of God's grace, we might be tempted to sin even more. If we sin willfully, thinking beforehand that God is obligated to forgive us, we lose the security we have in God.

What shall we say then? Shall we continue in sin that grace may abound? God forbid. -Romans 6:1

ETHICS OF THE BIBLE

We all need ethical teaching. Ethical teaching is necessary to strengthen our conscience against the eroding influences, of immorality, false teachings, and human rationalizations. Ethical teaching must coincide with our conscience if it is to be effective. If ethical teaching does not coincide with our conscience, it then becomes just something someone is trying to program into our minds.

All humans have a moral code written into their conscience. Everyone's behavior reveals this inborn code, no matter how much crooked thinking has been added to it. None of this moral code's directives can possibly stand on their own as a moral authority without the enforcement of God. Every unenforced rule is an absurdity. Suppose a teacher made the rule, do not cheat, but made no attempt to enforce this rule. He did not observe his students while they were taking tests and simply gave the highest grades to those with the most correct answers. Those who cheated were graduated and those who did not cheat were failed because their scores were lower. This example shows the absurdity of an unenforced rule.

The thought-out, reasoned attitude all true atheists should have is, "Why should I care about others, they're not me?" For a true atheist, nothing can be right, nothing can be wrong, nothing can be moral and nothing can be immoral. Who decrees what is wrong? Evolution? Our mothers? Our government? However, even professing atheists take our moral code seriously, which is a behavior that manifests a belief in God. Although they deny it, atheists show by their behavior they have God's existence written into their minds.

Sociologists often create hypothetical ethical situations, which are confusing because they omit important facts. Here is an example of their hypothetical situations: A person can choose to throw a railroad switch, which would send a train on its way to kill one person instead of the five it is on course to kill. What should he do?

The answer depends on the degree of certainty he has about each choice, which the sociologist has omitted. It is improbable that anyone can attain a high degree of certainty about either choice in a matter of seconds. This example continues with the option of throwing a large person onto the tracks to stop the train and save five people. Here, the degree of certainty that the large person will die is almost 100%, while the degree of certainty the other five will die is much less. Hypothetical ethical situations often omit facts, in this case, the degree of certainty for each choice.

God's Holy Spirit is the only morally good force in the world. God and His Holy Spirit are good because their commands are meant to keep us on the path of spiritual joy. The only morally good action we can take is to manifest God's Spirit. No action is good of itself but good only in obedience to God's command. It is impossible for us to do good without obedience to God's Law of Love in our heart. We can only do good when we allow the Holy Spirit to manifest love, joy, peace, longsuffering, gentleness, goodness, faith, meekness and temperance from our heart (Galatians 5:22). These are manifestations of God's Holy Spirit and not manifestations of our own selves.

For I know that in me (that is, in my flesh) dwells no good thing. −Romans 7:18

And Jesus said unto him, "Why do you call me good? There is none good but one, that is, God." −Mark 10:18

Jesus was perfect but not good. Jesus was perfect because he was perfectly obedient. The goodness that lived within Him was God's goodness.

We have this treasure (God's Spirit) in earthen vessels (our bodies) that the excellency of the power may be of God, and not of us. −II Corinthians 4:7

All things are lawful for me but all things edify not. −I Corinthians 10:23

Certain activities do not help anyone but in moderation, they do not hurt anyone. God allows these activities. For example, Jesus drank wine in moderation. However, even He was attacked for being a winebibber by religious hypocrites (Matthew 11:19). Jesus obviously drank alcoholic wine because it would have been ridiculous for the hypocrites to attack Him for drinking grape juice. Drinking in moderation is reasonable. The religious law, 'Do not drink,' is unreasonable.

Let your moderation be known unto all. −Philippians 4:5

In conclusion, ethics is not rationalizations that enable people to believe to be ethical whatever they wish to be ethical. Ethics has definite laws and a definite enforcer of those laws— God. If you examine the experiences your conscience provides, you will discover the laws of ethics for yourself.

FREEDOM OF RELIGION

An example of crooked thinking that promotes hypocrisy and that has been programmed into most people's mind is the belief that everyone is morally entitled to freedom of religion. Although everyone is legally entitled to freedom of religion, no one is morally entitled to it. Moral freedom of religion is actually the freedom to believe to be right whatever a person wishes to be right. It is the freedom from "right and wrong" and freedom from morality. It is the freedom to believe in religious legalisms, superstitions and absurdities. The concept of moral freedom of religion is what makes religious absurdities seem reasonable.

We do not have freedom of astronomy; reason will not allow us to believe that the earth is the center of the universe. We do not have freedom of geography; reason will not allow us to believe the earth is flat. We also do not have freedom of chemistry; reason will not allow us to believe that lead can be turned into gold. Reason discredited these absurdities centuries ago, but the freedom to believe in religious absurdities has not yet been discredited.

Do not confuse the legality of freedom of religion with the morality of freedom of religion. It should not be illegal to believe that the earth is the center of the universe and it should not be illegal to believe in religious absurdities. However, if civilization is to advance, the freedom to believe in religious absurdities needs to be discredited just as the freedom to believe in other absurdities has been.

THE PARADOX OF BEING BORN AGAIN

That which is born of the flesh is flesh, and that which is born of the Spirit is Spirit. Marvel not that I said unto you, you must be born again. –John 3:6, 7

A born again person is a spiritual paradox, having two opposite natures in the same body. These natures are the Spirit of God and the spirit of flesh (which is a paradox in itself). Everyone who is born again faces a daily battle because between two natures at war with each other. The flesh complains; the Spirit of God gives thanks. The flesh seeks excitement; the Spirit of God ministers rest. The flesh feeds on entertainment and pride; the Spirit of God feeds on love and exalting God. The flesh seeks its own welfare; the Spirit of God seeks the welfare of others. The flesh is fearful; the Spirit of God is at peace.

For he who sows to his flesh shall of the flesh reap corruption; but he who sows to the Spirit shall of the Spirit reap life everlasting. –Galatians 6:8

As long as we are on this earth, we will have a lower nature. We must live with it but we do *not* need to feed it. When the Apostle Paul wrestled with his lower nature, he came to a greater understanding of the power of God's deliverance.

For I know that in me (that is, in my flesh) dwells no good thing: for to will is present with me; but how to perform that which is good I find not. For the good that I would I do not: but the evil which I would not, that I do. Now if I do that I would not, it is no more I that do it, but sin that dwells in me. O wretched man that I am! Who shall deliver me from the body of this death? I thank God that He will through Jesus Christ Our Lord! –Romans 7:18-20, 24, 25

SECTION III - THE FOUR KEYS TO SPIRITUAL JOY

The Four Keys to Spiritual Joy will lead to the greatest experience a person can have. The greatest joy is the joy we receive when we realize how much God loves us and that He cares about everything we do. Sometimes it takes years of seeking until a person finds the joy of the "born again" experience and sometimes it only takes minutes to find it.

However, most people are not at all interested in spiritual joy. They have the joy of money or other joys of this world and they would never sacrifice those for spiritual joy. Nevertheless, if you decide to seek this deep eternal joy, I wish you success in finding it.

REPENTANCE

Repentance is the First Key to spiritual joy. If we are not experiencing joy, all we need to do is repent. Okay, it is not always that easy, but it can be. Finding the thoughts or actions keeping us from being joyful sometimes requires diligently seeking God. Is some thought keeping us from rejoicing and thanking God for another beautiful day? Then we need to repent of it. We are always responsible for our own unhappiness; we should never blame anyone else. Those who blame others become filled with bitterness. Forgiving others as well as being forgiven by God is part of the baptism of repentance. Forgiving everyone of *everything* brings tremendous joy. It is much easier to forgive when you remember even some of the things that God has forgiven you. Forgiveness, however, does not mean forgetting or stopping working or justice.

John baptized in the wilderness and preached the baptism of repentance for the forgiveness of sins. -Mark 1:4

50

From that time Jesus began to preach, *repent*: for the Kingdom of Heaven is at hand. –Matthew 4:17

Unfortunately, the message of repentance has been ridiculed more than any other teaching of the Bible. It is often associated with a wild-eyed fanatic picketing innocent bystanders. However, repentance is the first and most basic teaching of Jesus. We cannot become filled with joy and faith in God if we are already filled with other things.

Trying to enter into the joy of the Lord without repentance is the wide, smooth path to death warmed over and not the straight and narrow path to joy. Spiritual joy cannot be added to our carnal nature, it must replace our carnal nature. Trying to add spirituality to our carnal nature only results in hypocrisy. Growth in spiritual joy comes from repenting of more and more of our carnal nature.

Here are some important things from which to repent if we want the joy of salvation. (1) We need to repent of pride. Pride strangles people by keeping them from learning. When a proud person becomes mired in sin, it is almost impossible to help him out of it. His pride will not allow him to admit anything or learn anything. When we repent of pride and ask God for help, we can begin to realize just how much God loves us. (2) We need to repent of always wanting more, so we can remain in the joyous emotion of *thankfulness*. Thankfulness for everything is essential for joy. (3) We need to repent of our own will and accept God's Will as Jesus did when He prayed in the garden. We sometimes fear that our plan will not happen, but we need never fear that God's Plan will not happen. It always happens. We can rejoice when we realize that God's plan is always better than ours is. His plan always brings to pass our maximum joy. And (4) we need to repent of worldly busyness that keeps us from remembering that our names are written in heaven. Paul writes in I Corinthians 15:19 that if we forget about heaven we will be more miserable than anyone else will. These guidelines establish our foundation for joy.

Let us go on unto perfection, not laying again the foundation of repentance from dead works. –Hebrews 6:1

Not only is repentance from evil works necessary but also repentance from dead works. A dead work is any religious work that lacks both mercy and reason. Included in dead works are negative commands such as, "Don't do this," and, "Don't eat that." Following rules such as these is similar to trying to make a bad tree look good by picking off all its bad fruit. The tree will still be bad even though it has no bad fruit on it. God wants us to be new trees, filled with the fruits of the Holy Spirit and rooted in love. We can only accomplish this by repenting of even thinking about our carnal nature. We can then focus on others and do acts of mercy.

And now the axe is laid unto the root of the tree. Every tree that does not bear good fruit is cut down and cast into the fire. –Luke 3:9

Wherefore if you be dead with Christ from the rudiments of the world, why, as though living in the world are you subject to ordinances: Touch not; taste not; handle not. –Colossians 2:20, 21

Despise not the chastening of the Lord, For whom the Lord loves he chastens. –Hebrews12:5, 6

We can never find the joy of the Lord if we refuse to be disciplined by God. Discipline brings repentance. Discipline is certainly not joyous at the time it is given. However, if we accept God's discipline we can become His child and live in His joy.

God is so loving He will *always* remind us when we are not on the spiritual path. He reminds us by giving us emotional pain. Emotional pain and physical pain both have the same purpose. They both are warnings that something is not right.

As many as I love, I rebuke and chasten: be zealous therefore and repent. –Revelation 3:19

Happy is the man God corrects. –Job 5:17

Incredibly, sorrow is a building block in the foundation for joy. Godly sorrow is necessary for repentance (II Corinthians 7:10). When we experience godly sorrow, we need to seek the Lord and repent of what He is telling us needs to change. Repentance brings joy.

There is joy in heaven every time a sinner repents (Luke 15:10). However, we will not find our greatest joy at the time of our repentance. We will obtain that when we make it all the way back to our Father in heaven, as the prodigal son did. Then we will understand more of the tremendous love our Father in heaven has for us.

LOVE

Love is the Second Key to spiritual joy because acts of love enable us to experience this joy. Now, the new commandment is to love our neighbor as Jesus loves us. Jesus has a purpose in commanding us to love one another. He wants us to be full of joy. Yes, love and joy go hand in hand. If we say we love someone and do not have joy, then we do not understand love as Jesus taught it.

These things (loving one another) have I spoken unto you that my joy might remain in you and that your joy might be full.—John 15:11

Is it possible to love everyone we meet and still be full of joy? The answer is yes, if we are smart and spiritually strong. Love is not syrupy sweet or blindly sacrificing. Love is wise enough to empathize and strong enough to comfort, encourage or rebuke.

Some people are confused because the word love has many different meanings as it is used in the English language. It is even used to describe two opposite emotions—selfishness and unselfishness. The word "love" is used to describe selfishness as in, "I love money." The word "love" is also used in the Bible to describe unselfish giving to others. The primary reason people are not full of love is that they have not understood the importance of learning how to love. That is right—love is something we learn. Children, for example, are usually excited to talk at great lengths about themselves and about what they are doing. As they grow older they learn to love, that is, they learn to allow others to talk more while they talk less about themselves.

But go and learn what this means, I will have mercy and not sacrifice. —Matthew 9:13

When Jesus specifically tells us to learn something, it is a good idea for us to learn it. He wants us to learn the difference between showing mercy and making sacrifices. This is the difference between love and hypocrisy, between joy and deadness, between life and death.

No one is born with the strength or the wisdom needed to love. Our ability to love grows through prayer, studying the scriptures and seeking God in every difficult situation. Learning to love involves seeking God, finding Him, listening to Him and then gaining the strength to follow Him. We need to take the time to find God and get to know Him as our Father because God's love extends to every detail of our life.

Some people live their entire lives never loving anybody. They never gain the strength to speak what others need to hear. Instead, they will speak only what others want to hear. Some common actions these people use to cover up this lack of love are flattery or the giving of gifts. These actions appear good but are empty of honesty and love.

Not everyone who says to me, Lord, Lord, shall enter into the kingdom of heaven; but he that does the will of my Father which is in heaven. —Matthew 7:21

Learning to love is necessary for fellowship with God. Unfortunately, some people are not willing to learn to love because they are afraid of the demands love might make on them. Others have good intentions but lack humility, understanding or the strength to love. Additionally, some do not love their neighbor because they think he or she does not deserve it. *Nobody* deserves love, but to be happy we need to love others.

Let us *not* love in word, *nor* in tongue, but in deed and in truth. –I John 3:18

This is an interesting and often overlooked verse about love. This verse states that we should *not* say we love someone but rather we should show love instead. At first, this sounds shocking—not saying, "I love you." But think about it. Saying we love someone is really boasting about ourselves. The fact the person you are talking to wishes it be true and, therefore, believes it to be true has made this boasting socially acceptable. Imagine a world in which hypocrites, liars and those wishing to take advantage of others were deprived of credibility when they said, "I love you." I John 3:18 is trying to establish the credibility of actions over words. Remember, you are the judge of whether or not someone loves you. When someone says, "I love you," is that person being boastful or has that person really learned what love is?

Love works no ill to his neighbor, therefore love is the fulfilling of the law. –Romans 13:10

Doing acts of compassion from the heart fulfills everything God commands. It is mercy and compassion that fulfill all laws. It is not the keeping of certain laws that fulfills our obligation to love. When we follow the laws and traditions of men, we become focused on ourselves. Am I properly dressed? Is my diet correct? Am I doing the right thing at the right time? The laws of men demand we look at ourselves. This not only quenches the Spirit of God but kills our joy as well. The letter of the law brings death, but the Spirit (of love) gives life (II Corinthians 3:6).

When we focus on ourselves, it is impossible for us to perform acts of compassion for someone else. Religious rules demand that we look at ourselves but the law of love demands that we look to others. Love begins by looking to our neighbor, doing acts of compassion for him, and helping him experience joy. Love equals joy.

FAITH IN GOD'S WORD

Faith in God's Word is the Third Key to spiritual joy. We need to (1) trust that God has created a path of joy for us and (2) ask Him to help us find that path. It is necessary to have faith in God's promises in order to live continually in joy. If God did not help us, as He promises, the path of joy would not exist. God will do everything necessary for us to remain in His joy.

We cannot successfully overcome the obstacles of life by ourselves. We need to ask and trust God to help us. Trusting in money, which many people do, will help in overcoming some obstacles but not all of them. Death, for example, is one obstacle that money cannot overcome. Money might help postpone death, but it will never help to overcome it.

True faith is more than just hope. It is a belief in God's Word. We cannot work up faith or generate it by an act of our own will. God gives us a deeper and greater faith when we study the scriptures and fill our heart with His Word. Biblical teachings are essential for building faith. True faith is faith in God's heaven. It is saying, "I want to do more acts of mercy in order to get an even greater joy." It is saying, "I will be happy to leave this world to be with Jesus in heaven, but until I go I will continue to store more treasures there." When we completely trust God about His path of joy for us, we will say, "I want for my life whatever God wants for my life."

The more experiences that we have in applying the Word of God to our life, the more faith in God we will have. The manifestation of our faith in God is shown by our love and depth of our spiritual rest. God will keep us in perfect peace when we have complete faith in Him (Isaiah 26:3).

So then faith comes by hearing, and hearing by the Word of God. –Romans 10:17

For in Christ Jesus neither circumcision avails anything, nor uncircumcision: but faith which works by love. –Galatians 5:6

Above all, taking the shield of faith, Wherewith you shall be able to quench all the fiery darts of the wicked. –Ephesians 6:16

Certainly, the lies of the wicked are among the worst of the fiery darts. Satan's lies have interrupted everyone's joy at one time or another. The shield of faith in God's Word is the perfect protection against these lies. The stronger we are established in Truth the less we will be hurt by the lies of the wicked.

God is the only one worthy of our trust. No one else will constantly have our best interests at heart, only God. Trusting others completely is often a mistake.

Thus saith the Lord; Cursed be the man who trusts in man and trusts in an arm of flesh. –Jeremiah 17:5

Think. If we devoted our life to the cause of righteousness and God did not do anything for us, God would be unfair. However, God is more than fair with everyone. He will give us everything we need to continue our work. Have faith in Him.

Every gift of God and every type of miracle is available from God if we can only believe. No matter what situation we are in, the Hand of God is able to reach down and save us. Furthermore, we are not limited by our environment; we are not limited by our education; we are not limited by what we have accomplished in the past. Our only limitation is what we believe. Consequently, THE *ONLY* THING WE WILL EVER NEED IS FAITH IN GOD'S WORD!

BECOMING BORN AGAIN

Becoming born again is the Fourth Key to spiritual joy. When we become born again of God's Spirit we will be headed toward uninterrupted, eternal joy. Thanks be to God for that! We may lose our joy for a time in this world but once we are born again, God will always bring us back to that narrow path of spiritual joy.

Modern Christianity talks much of accepting Jesus and being born again. What does it mean to accept Jesus? To a Baptist it means one thing, to a Pentecostal something else and to a Catholic it means yet something different. What does it mean to be born again? Those who are born again will not be rooted in this world but rooted in love instead. John 3:8 reveals every one who is born again of God's Spirit is like the wind because they are all rooted in love, instead of this world.

Accepting and receiving Jesus is more than repeating the words, "I accept Jesus," and then becoming a churchgoer. Accepting Jesus does not mean blindly accepting a religious leader to be your lord or copying all the mannerisms of a particular congregation. Accepting Jesus means accepting *all* His teachings and accepting *all* His actions, the things He does in your life. When we accept Jesus with all our heart mind and soul, He will put His transforming Spirit within us. We will be transformed because we will gain the ability to rejoice when we extend God's love to others. Many churchgoers who now claim to be born again have no idea what being born again means. They have merely paid a preacher to tell them that they are born again. They are what I call "99 per centers" because they believe 99 per cent of the Bible. Nevertheless, it is the last one per cent of the Bible, which they refuse to believe that would humble them and break their will. When we allow our will to be broken, we are forced to embrace God's Will. It is only then that we are able to obtain the great "born again" joy.

They that fall upon the Rock shall be broken; but those upon whom the Rock falls will be ground to powder. –Matthew 21:44

Jesus answered and said unto him, Verily, verily I say unto you, Except a man be born again he cannot see the kingdom of God. –John 3:3

The ultimate experience of a joy-filled life is to become born again of God's Spirit. So what is being born again? The term born again has been used in describing many different experiences. A puzzled Nicodemus asked, "How is it possible for an old man to enter into his mother's womb and be born a second time?"(John 3:4)

The parable Jesus told about a prodigal son best explains being born again. The prodigal son obtained what would have been his inheritance from his father and quickly wasted it all on riotous living. He became so destitute that he even thought of eating pigs' food. He came to his senses and repented of his wayward lifestyle. He decided to seek his father and confess his sin to him, hoping his father would, at least, receive him as a servant. Upon seeing his son, the father rejoiced and received his lost son unconditionally. (Luke 15:11-32)

The analogy to being born again begins when the prodigal son experienced a godly sorrow, which led to his repentance. Even though the angels in heaven rejoiced when he repented, he did not yet receive the joy of salvation. He received that when he found his father and realized how much his father loved him. This rejoicing represents the fulfillment of the true born again experience.

We can experience the joy of salvation for ourselves. We merely need to let God transform us as the prodigal son did. If we pray, "God, be merciful to me, a sinner." Or, "God, please save me." (Luke 18:13), our Father in heaven will hear us and feed us with love and joy. The vital prerequisite to becoming born again is telling God that we need His help and then allowing Him to solve our problems His way. The realization that God really loves us and is concerned about every detail of our lives brings the deepest joy and peace that we could possibly experience.

Incidentally, the prodigal son seemingly made it back to his father immediately. In our lives, however, it may take many years to overcome the multitude of obstacles that bad religionists use to hinder us from finding God and the born again joy.

Once we realize we are going to live forever, every experience we then have can be seen in the light of the permanent, uninterrupted joy that awaits us. Our new life is similar to a basketball game with the final score fixed in our favor. Victory may seem far away, but God's final triumph is certain.

Whenever we need to renew our joy, we can always stop for a few minutes and concentrate on the fact that God has written our name in heaven. We can now pause at any time and rejoice in the mercy that we have received from God. Remember: All is well that ends in rejoicing.

Rejoice because your name is written in heaven. –Luke 10:20

IN CONCLUSION

This book started with essays on the scientific discovery of God. It went on to give insightful essays from Christian Objectivism. It concluded with the Four Keys to Spiritual Joy.

These essays are strong enough to destroy atheism as well as enable you to experience the depths of spiritual joy for yourself. I hope you use this information wisely and achieve the highest quality of life possible. God has a beautiful path, full of joy, prepared for each one of us. However, it is up to us to seek that path until we find it.

The Four Keys to Spiritual Joy unlock the hidden treasures of life. Repentance is the first key because we first need to stop doing or thinking the thing making us unhappy. Love is the second key because acts of love bring spiritual joy. Faith in God's Word is the third key because, without that faith, we cannot continue a life of love and, thus, a life of spiritual joy. Becoming born again of God's Spirit is the fourth key because when we allow God to transform us with His Spirit we will always be headed to uninterrupted, eternal joy. Praise the Lord Jesus Christ for that!

Talk to God about everything. Be reasonable and think for yourself. Trust your own thinking abilities. Be an individual because you are a minority of one. Be true to your conscience, the voice of Jesus, because you are the only you in existence. No one else can live the life God has ordained for you.

Remember that life in this world will never be perfect, but this world is less than one second compared to what comes after it. And what comes after this world will be perfect!

Wisdom is the principal thing; therefore get wisdom. −Proverbs 4:7

Now the God of hope fill you with all joy and peace in believing, that you may abound in hope, through the power of the Holy Ghost. −Romans 15:13

ABOUT THE AUTHOR

Eric Demaree obtained a degree in philosophy from Western Illinois University in 1973. He has retired from being a letter carrier in the U. S. Postal Service. For the past 40 years, he has worked with many different ministries in the western USA and the Philippines, where he has made more than twenty missionary trips.

He has been the Director of the oldest local ministry in Las Vegas, NV—the God-in-me Ministries. In the Philippines he taught "Values" classes in the public schools, worked with government social workers and co-pastored a small church.

If you have any comments or questions, you may contact me, Eric Demaree at moral.arg1@yahoo.com

If you enjoyed this book, help others to find it by leaving a comment or review on Amazon.com (Search—The Argument From Human Behavior)